WIT & WISDOM FROM THE ROCKET MAN

Published in 2022 by OH!
An Imprint of Welbeck Non-Fiction Limited,
part of Welbeck Publishing Group.
Based in London and Sydney.
www.welbeckpublishing.com

Compilation text © Welbeck Non-Fiction Limited 2022
Design © Welbeck Non-Fiction Limited 2022

ISBN 978-1-80069-231-2

Compilation and Design: RH
Editorial: Lisa Dyer
Project manager: Russell Porter
Production: Jess Brisley

A CIP catalogue record for this book is available from the British Library

Printed in China

10 9 8 7 6 5 4 3 2 1

Illustrations: Shutterstock.com

THE LITTLE GUIDE TO

ELTON JOHN

WIT & WISDOM FROM
THE ROCKET MAN

CONTENTS

INTRODUCTION — 6

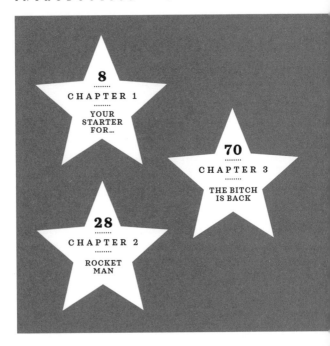

8
....
CHAPTER 1
....
YOUR
STARTER
FOR...

28
....
CHAPTER 2
....
ROCKET
MAN

70
....
CHAPTER 3
....
THE BITCH
IS BACK

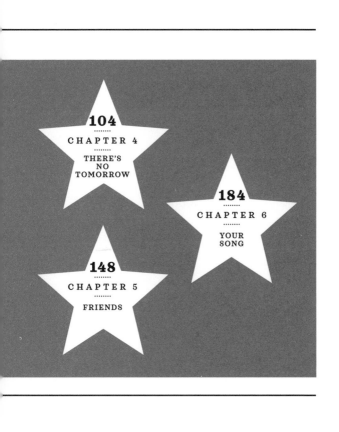

104

CHAPTER 4

THERE'S
NO
TOMORROW

184

CHAPTER 6

YOUR
SONG

148

CHAPTER 5

FRIENDS

INTRODUCTION

Sir Elton Hercules John has enjoyed a phenomenal career filled with success, excess and achievement. His "farewell" tour was announced as more than 300 dates across all corners of the globe, but nobody really believes he will stop touring, do they? Illness, COVID-19 and other circumstances conspired to drag it out even longer, but the Farewell Yellow Brick Road Tour concerts have sold out everywhere as fans take what could well be their final opportunity to see this unique artist live on stage. Elton John is still a musical and cultural phenomenon, more than 50 years after the start of his incredible career.

Exploding onto the music scene in the 1970s, Elton took the world by storm and enjoyed stunning success in the charts — particularly in the US where he had seven consecutive No. 1 albums in little over three years — but the music created by him, alongside the words of lyricist Bernie Taupin, is famous everywhere.

This little book celebrates the career, music and character of one of the most original, popular, interesting, colourful, engaging and outspoken musicians ever to take to the stage.

And what he says is certainly entertaining. Intelligent, erudite, witty, charming and at times downright bitchy, Elton's words make for great reading. His emotions run close to the surface so he reveals a lot about his fascinating life behind the scenes. Elton is not known for holding back, and many of his own wise, hilarious and wickedly cutting words of wisdom (and humour) are included, as well as reactions from his numerous friends, commentators and even enemies. On these pages you will also discover highlights of his amazing career and record-breaking achievements, in music and farther afield. Some of his greatest songs are discussed, as well as his work with talented collaborators over the years (Lady Gaga, George Michael, Eminem, Dua Lipa, to name a few). Elton's charitable work is observed, including his own AIDS Foundation and other initiatives.

Whether you are a fan of Elton from back in the day, you discovered his beautiful music from his stunning '80s resurgence or whether you're just curious to learn more about a musical treasure, this book will feed your hunger for all things Elton.

CHAPTER
ONE

Your Starter For...

From Reginald Dwight to
Elton Hercules John.

Reginald Kenneth Dwight was born in Pinner, England on March 25,

1947

to Stanley and Sheila Eileen Dwight.

> **He gave me the determination to make something of myself.**

Elton John on his father,
interview with Terry Gross, 2019

Source: npr.org

At the age of

11

Reg Dwight won a scholarship to the Royal Academy of Music in London. He left before taking his final exams.

66

My childhood really shaped
the way I became as an artist,
because I was determined
to prove myself to my father
... I didn't need to prove
anything to myself; I just
wanted to prove something
to him.

99

Elton John, interview with Melena Ryzik, 2019

Source: nytimes.com

"Come Back Baby" (1965)

♪

Recorded with Bluesology, written by Elton John

♪

Released as a single in 1965

♪

Elton's first professional recording contract was with the band Bluesology

Both Elton and
Bernie Taupin
answered an ad in
the *New Musical
Express* in 1967,
headed "Liberty
Wants Talent".

"

Lincolnshire is the Idaho of England. You were either going to drive a tractor for the rest of your life or head for the city to work in a factory. Answering a magazine ad placed by a new record company looking for talent was a form of desperation.

"

Bernie Taupin to Cal Fussman, 2012

Source: esquire.com

"

Our relationship has always been something that I don't think anybody can truly define. I don't think anybody will ever understand it 100 per cent.

"

Bernie Taupin

Source: people.com

66

He's probably more important than me when it comes to writing the songs, because he has to write the words before I write the music.

99

Elton John introduces Bernie Taupin,
The Arsenio Hall Show, 1992

Source: youtube.com

66

When Elton and I started out,
we were literally kids.
Then we became young adults.
Then we became adults.
Now we're old men.
But old men with distinctly
young ideas.

99

Bernie Taupin to Cal Fussman, 2012

Source: esquire.com

66

From the time we met, we
were pretty much inseparable.
We were all each other had.

99

Bernie Taupin

Source: people.com

Elton's debut album, *Empty Sky*, was released in the UK in

1969

but it was not released in the USA until 1975.

66

... the way we write songs is very eerie as well. We're not in the same room. I don't have a melody — I'm inspired by him.

99

Elton John on Bernie Taupin,
interview with Melena Ryzik, 2019

Source: nytimes.com

66

I don't need to try to figure
out why it works.
We never question that.
We just continue.

99

Bernie Taupin on Elton John,
interview with Melena Ryzik, 2019

Source: nytimes.com

"

They [Bernie Taupin and
Elton John] had written
something like 20 songs
before they had even met.

"

Tom Doyle, *Captain Fantastic: Elton John's Stellar
Trip Through the '70s*, 2017

Source: biography.com

Elton's first US album, *Elton John*, was nominated for a Grammy Award in

1971

but lost to *Bridge Over Troubled Water*.

"

... all Elton and Bernie wanted
to be were songwriters. They
didn't think about going on the
road and making all of these
albums and playing arenas
and stadiums and, you know ...
what's happened since.

"

Nigel Olsson, interview with Joe Bosso in
Music Radar, 2011

Source: musicradar.com

66

When you work with
somebody as talented
as Elton, you've got to be
prepared for, 'Well, this is
what I want do to'.

99

Davey Johnstone, interview with Russell Leadbetter
in *The Herald*, 2017

Source: heraldscotland.com

CHAPTER
TWO

Rocket Man

Elton is suddenly catapulted
to stardom in the UK, USA and
around the world.

"

Elton John is a fast worker.
He just about has to be
because he allows himself
only ten days to write and
rehearse all the material
before recording an album.

"

Steve Turner, interview with Elton John, 1973

Source: rocksbackpages.com

Elton lived with his mother and stepfather in an apartment until he had four albums simultaneously in the US Top 40.

"

Rejoice! Rock music has a new star.

"

Robert Hilburn on Elton at The Troubadour,
Los Angeles Times, 1970

Source: latimes.com

"

I was the quintessential country bumpkin and he was sophisticated. He lived in London and played in clubs!

"

Bernie Taupin, *Daily Mail*, 2019

Source: mailonline.com

Elton wrote the music for "Your Song" in 1969 (lyrics by Bernie Taupin). It was released on the 1970 album *Elton John.*

"Your Song" (1970)

♪

Recorded in 1970 in Trident Studios, London

♪

Originally the b-side to "Take Me to the Pilot" in the USA

♪

"Your Song" has never topped the charts

"

It was one of the first songs
we wrote, when we really got
locked into writing.

"

Bernie Taupin, on "Your Song", 2009

Source: americansongwriter.com

"Your Song" was
inducted to the
Grammy Hall of
Fame in

1971

> **"**
>
> I thought, 'F**k, the chorus had better be something special when it finally arrives.'
>
> **"**

Elton John to Bob Dylan, on "Tiny Dancer",
interview with Alexis Petridis, 2019

Source: theguardian.com

"Tiny Dancer"
(1972)

♪

Certified platinum in the UK despite never having been released there as a single

♪

The song is seven times platinum in Australia

♪

First released on the album *Madman Across the Water*

Elton's fourth album, *Friends*, was a film soundtrack released in 1971. It became his third gold record in the USA in three months that year.

Source: variety.com

Rumour has it
that at one point
during the 1970s
Elton John's record
sales accounted
for two per cent
of all records sold
worldwide.

Source: udiscovermusic.com

66

We both had tremendous
trauma in our lives,
to be quite honest. I can't
think of any real major artists
that probably hasn't. I had
addictions of my own —
I wasn't any fairy-tale prince.

99

Bernie Taupin, interview with Melena Ryzik, 2019

Source: nytimes.com

"Rocket Man" (1972)

♪

The full title of the song is "Rocket Man (I Think It's Going to Be a Long, Long Time)"

♪

The lyrics were inspired by Ray Bradbury's *The Rocket Man*

♪

The song peaked at No. 2 in the UK charts, No. 6 in the US and No. 13 in Australia

Elton's ninth album, *Captain Fantastic and the Brown Dirt Cowboy* was the first ever to debut at

No. 1

on the USA album charts (May 1975).

> 66
>
> Every lyric was about
> Bernie and me, about our
> experiences ... I was in
> love with Bernie, not in a
> sexual way, but because he
> was the person I was looking
> for my entire life...
>
> 99

Elton John on *Captain Fantastic
and the Brown Dirt Cowboy*, *Rolling Stone*, 2013

Source: rollingstone.com

"

It's three or four weeks long,
which is long for me.

"

Elton John on his UK tour,
interview with Bob Harris, 1973

Source: youtube.com

"

The last time I have to sing 'Crocodile Rock', I will probably throw a party.

"

Elton John, *Deeney Talks* podcast, 2021

Source: shows.acast.com

"

It's ridiculous,
he has written four songs
in a day sometimes.

"

Bernie on Elton, 2009

Source: americansongwriter.com

"

But English people, English entertainers, have always been very flamboyant. And I think it's because of the music hall tradition that we have in England.

"

Elton John, interview with Terry Gross, 2019

Source: npr.org

"Goodbye Yellow Brick Road" (1973)

♪

The title track from Elton's bestselling 1973 album

♪

Recording for the song (and album) was moved to France, after starting in Jamaica

♪

Elton performed the song on *The Muppet Show* in 1978

"Saturday Night's Alright For Fighting" (1973)

♪

First single release from
Goodbye Yellow Brick Road

♪

Has been covered by
Nickelback, Queen and
The Who, among others

♪

One of Elton's most-played songs
live — an estimated 1,800 times

66

Elton rattled off superbly
insensitive knees-up versions
of his work, pub standards,
Christmas songs and even
Bob Dylan.

99

John Walters, *Radio Times*, 1983

Source: peel.fandom.com

"

We decided, why don't we start our own label?

"

Elton John interview with Bob Harris, 1973

Source: youtube.com

"The Bitch Is Back" (1974)

♪

From the album *Carabou*, recorded on Carabou Ranch

♪

Lyrics were inspired by Taupin's wife, who used the phrase when Elton was in a bad mood*

♪

Some US radio stations refused to play it because of the title

*Source: Elizabeth J. Rosenthal, *His Song: The Musical Journey of Elton John*, 2001

John Lennon played with Elton John on stage at Madison Square Garden in New York in 1974, including the single, "Whatever Gets You Through the Night", which featured Elton on piano and vocals.

"Bennie and the Jets" (1974)

♪

The applause at the start was taken from the crowd at Jimi Hendrix's Isle of Wight performance

♪

The song is also written as "Benny and the Jets".

66

The whole idea of "Bennie and the Jets" was almost Orwellian, you know — it was supposed to be futuristic.

99

Bernie Taupin to Cal Fussman, 2012

Source: esquire.com

"Candle in the Wind" (1974)

♪

Originally about Marilyn Monroe, the song was re-written in 1997 as a tribute to Diana, Princess of Wales

♪

The single release in 1974 featured "Bennie and the Jets" on the b-side

Elton played "Candle in the Wind" at Princess Diana's funeral in 1997 to an estimated TV audience of 2.5bn.

66

Solzhenitsyn had written a
book called *Candle in the
Wind* ... I thought, what a
great way of describing
someone's life.

99

Bernie Taupin, *Mojo*, 2019

Source: mojo4music.com

66

There's nothing wrong with going to bed with somebody of your own sex. I think everybody's bisexual to a certain degree. I don't think it's just me.

99

Elton John, *Rolling Stone*, 1976

Source: rollingstone.com

"

I've hopefully got two or three
years left where I can have a
good time...

"

Elton John on *Parkinson*, 1976

Source: youtube.com

"Sorry Seems to Be the Hardest Word" (1976)

♪

Released as a single and on the album *Blue Moves*

♪

Gold certified in the USA, with more than 1m sales

♪

Elton also recorded the song with the band Blue, in 2002

"Don't Go Breaking My Heart" (1976)

♪

Recorded with Kiki Dee, lyrics and music are by Elton and Bernie Taupin

♪

Won the Ivor Novello Award for Best Pop Song in 1977

♪

Following this, Elton did not have a solo chart-topping single in the UK until 1990's "Sacrifice"

19

official versions
of "Don't Go
Breaking My Heart"
have been released.

Source: eltonjohn.com

"Don't Go Breaking My Heart" is sampled on the 1997 Daft Punk track "Phoenix" from their debut album *Homework*.

Source: whosampled.com

"

I don't think I've been put on Earth just to play music and write songs. I have a feeling that I've got to do something else in life as well.

"

Elton John interview with Jenny Baxter
in *Talk*, 1990

"

It took a fairly Herculean
effort to get yourself noticed
for taking too much cocaine
in the music industry of
1970s LA, but I was clearly
prepared to put the hours in.

"

Elton John, *The Observer*, 2019

Source: theguardian.com

"

I have made a decision tonight this is going to be the last show, alright?
So, er there's a lot more to me than playing on the road, and this is the last one I'm going to do...

"

Elton John live at Wembley Stadium, 1977

Source: youtube.com

CHAPTER
THREE

The Bitch Is Back

After a two-year break,
the songs, records and
performances keep coming.

Elton performed a
concert in front of

400,000

fans in New York's
Central Park in 1980.

> I hated my addiction. I hated the way I behaved. I hated how I treated people. I hated what I'd become. But I'm grateful that I had it because then I learned how to become who I am now.

Elton John, interview with Terry Gross, 2019

Source: npr.org

"Empty Garden (Hey Hey Johnny)" (1982)

♪

Written 18 months after the murder of John Lennon

♪

Elton played the song on *Saturday Night Live* in 1982

♪

The song is on Elton's 1982 album *Jump Up!*

Elton performed "Empty Garden (Hey Hey Johnny)" in New York in 1982 with Yoko Ono and John's son Sean Lennon.

66

When I met him I don't think
he actually knew who I was.

99

Elton John on President Reagan,
Parkinson in Australia, 1982

Source: youtube.com

66

I made a hell of a lot of money ... I voted socialist at the last election, then the Conservatives got in and lowered the tax rate to 60 per cent.

99

Elton John, interview with Lisa Robinson, 1982

Source: *The Inside Track* radio show

"

I'm a chameleon, I change
my colours all the time ...
I don't really think of my
image, actually.

"

Elton John on *Time and Again*, MSNBC News, 1982

Source: youtube.com

"I'm Still Standing" (1983)

♪

Taken from the album
Too Low for Zero

♪

Video was shot in Cannes and
Nice on the French coast

♪

Went platinum in Australia and
the UK, and gold in the USA

"

I was Elton John.
I had everything that
money could buy, but I was
really unhappy.

"

Elton John on
The Tomorrow Show with Tom Snyder, 1981

Source: youtube.com

80

"I Guess That's Why They Call It the Blues" (1983)

♪

Stevie Wonder plays harmonica

♪

Video was directed by Russell Mulcahy, who made more than 20 videos for Elton

♪

Too Low for Zero was Elton's bestselling album of the '80s

66

I don't do interviews with the press very much ... You think you've given them some good stuff, and then you read about all they want to know is about sex life, or hair transplant or the shoes and the glasses.

99

Elton John on *Time and Again*, MSNBC News, 1982

Source: youtube.com

66

You can call me a fat,
balding, talentless old queen
who can't sing, but you can't
tell lies about me.

99

Elton John, 1987

Source: theguardian.com

Elton John Top Ten Albums

10. *Too Low for Zero* (1983)

9. *Rock of the Westies* (1976)

8. *Elton John* (1970)

7. *17-11-70* (1971)

6. *Don't Shoot Me I'm Only the Piano Player* (1973)

5. *Honky Château* (1972)

4. *Tumbleweed Connection* (1970)

3. *Captain Fantastic and the Brown Dirt Cowboy* (1975)

2. *Madman Across the Water* (1971)

1. *Goodbye Yellow Brick Road* (1973)

Source: rollingstone.com reader's poll, 2013

In 1984 on
Valentine's Day,
Elton married
Renate Blauel. They
divorced in 1988.

66

And I loved Renate. She's a
great girl. I really, really loved
her. But, you know ... it is one
of the things I regret most in
my life, hurting her.

99

Elton John, interview in *The Australian*, 2008

Source: smoothradio.com

In 1985 Elton performed at Live Aid in London's Wembley Stadium.

Elton's Live Aid Setlist

1. "I'm Still Standing"

2. "Bennie and the Jets"

3. "Rocket Man"

4. "Don't Go Breaking My Heart" (with Kiki Dee)

5. "Don't Let the Sun Go Down on Me" (with Wham!)

6. "Can I Get a Witness"

"

Can anyone do anything about the wind in Hyde Park?

"

Elton John, phoning reception in his hotel, 1987

Source: theguardian.com

Elton John singles
have spent

444

weeks in the
UK charts.

Source: officialcharts.com

66

You looked like the f**king Queen Mother when you were on stage, where did you get that absolutely awful hat?

99

Freddie Mercury to Elton John,
backstage at Live Aid, 1985

Source: theguardian.com

> 66
>
> ... it's been an incredible journey playing with Elton ... You start out with somebody and you hope it'll last a year. Forty years and more, you never consider that.
>
> 99

Nigel Olsson, interview with Joe Bosso, 2011

Source: musicradar.com

"

Unless you show off, you're
not going to get noticed.

"

Elton John on *Fresh Air with Terry Gross*, 2013

Source: npr.org

66

The best awards are the
actual sales, because it means
the general public have
bought them, which is lovely.

99

Elton John, *Wogan*, 1986

Source: youtube.com

In 1976, Elton John became chairman of Watford FC, his lifelong football club. By 1983, the team were at the top of the First Division.

66

One learned to take defeat
quite well.

99

Elton John on Watford FC, interview with Paula
Yates, *The Tube*, 1986

Source: youtube.com

"

What the hell are you
thinking? Ridiculous. Makes
you look like a bloody fool.
Get rid of it.

"

Prince Philip to Elton John, on the subject of John's
car that was painted in the Watford FC colours,
circa 1976

Source: dailymail.co.uk

> **"**
> It's in my heart, my soul,
> you can't get rid of it.
> My passion for this club
> has never died and I'm so
> proud of this club.
> **"**

Elton John to Watford FC, 2021

Source: watfordfc.com

In 1987 Elton had surgery on his throat and cancelled his entire tour that year.

66

We did the operation in
Australia and it lowered
the timbre of my voice. It's
deeper, has more resonance
and it's stronger.

99

Elton John

Source: femalefirst.co.uk

101

"Sacrifice" (1989)

♪

Originally released in 1989, it was not until a 1990 re-release that it was a commercial success

♪

Elton John's first No. 1 single in France

♪

Certified gold in Australia

"Sacrifice" was Elton John's first solo No. 1 single — in 1990.

CHAPTER
FOUR

There's No Tomorrow

From the 1990s, Elton continues his amazing work, musically and behind the scenes for charity.

"

Music has healing power.
It has the ability to take
people out of themselves
for a few hours.

"

Elton John, interview with Jake Shears, 2006

Source: theguardian.com

Elton John's annual Academy Awards Viewing Party has raised more than $200m for the Elton John AIDS Foundation.

Source: variety.com

One of the top philanthropists in the UK, Elton supports at least 64 charities, including the Children's Tumor Foundation, Breast Cancer Research and the Starkey Hearing Foundation.

"Can You Feel the Love Tonight" (1994)

♪

Written with Tim Rice for the movie *The Lion King*

♪

Winner of an Academy Award, Golden Globe and Grammy Award

♪

Gold in the UK, France and Australia; platinum in the US

66

Look at you, it looks
like Dusty Springfield in a
nightmare.

99

Elton John to Rod Stewart

Source: bbc.com

66

Best f**king live act?
F**k off! ... That's me off her
f**ing Christmas card list..

99

Elton John on Madonna, Q Awards, 2004

Source: youtube.com

Elton John's Rocket Hour podcast has run for more than 300 episodes over six years.

66

I think performers
are all show-offs anyway,
especially musicians.

99

Elton John on *Fresh Air with Terry Gross*, 2013

Source: npr.org

"

Better to build bridges
than a wall.

"

Elton John, interview with Philip Galanes, 2014

Source: nytimes.com

66

Once you have people around
you who don't question you,
you're in a dangerous place.

99

Elton John, 2013

Source: huffingtonpost.com

"

I'm so angry.
I'm livid about what the
government did when
Brexit happened.
They made no provision
for the entertainment
business, and not just for

musicians, actors and film directors, but for the crews, the dancers, the people who earn a living by going to Europe.

Elton John, interview with Jude Rogers, 2021

Source: theguardian.com

Elton John Top Ten Songs

10. "Someone Saved My Life Tonight" (1975)

9. "Your Song" (1970)

8. "Daniel" (1973)

7. "Sorry Seems to Be the Hardest Word" (1974)

6. "Saturday Night's Alright for Fighting" (1973)

5. "Rocket Man (I Think It's Going to Be a Long, Long Time)" (1972)

4. "Captain Fantastic and the Brown Dirt Cowboy" (1975)

3. "Bennie and the Jets" (1974)

2. "Tiny Dancer" (1972)

1. "Goodbye Yellow Brick Road" (1973)

Source: ultimateclassicrock.com

> ""
> I am the most well-known
> homosexual in the world.
> ""

Elton John

Source: azquotes.com

Elton and his husband David Furnish were one of the first couples to register for a civil partnership in the UK — on the day the Act became law, in 2005.

"

I've been very privileged
because I'm in a business that
kind of accepts gay people.

"

Elton John

Source: variety.com

66

I actually think the gay
community will be quite
surprised by quite how gay
it feels.

99

Taron Egerton on *Rocketman*, 2019

Source: mtv.com

"

I know I'm an oddball to
have never felt any shame
about who I am, to have
never felt any fear.

"

Elton John, interview with Jude Rogers, 2021

Source: theguardian.com

> **"**
> I'm gay and I'm proud.
> **"**

Elton John, British LGBT Awards, 2020

Source: standard.co.uk

> **"**
>
> ... Jesus was a compassionate, super-intelligent gay man who understood human problems.
>
> **"**

Elton John, *Parade*, 2010

Source: chron.com

> **It's wonderful to be gay.
> I love being gay.
> I really do.**

Elton John, *Variety*, 2019

Source: variety.com

"

One of the best songs ever written...

"

Elton John on the Metallica song "Nothing Else Matters", on *The Howard Stern Show*, 2021

Source: youtube.com

66

After the tour finishes,
I'm very much looking
forward to closing off that
chapter of my life by saying
farewell to life on the road.
I need to dedicate more time
to raising my children.

99

Elton John on the Farewell Yellow Brick Road tour,
2019

"

I don't shave my testicles;
I use a cream you can
buy in France.

"

Elton John on *Friday Night with Jonathan Ross*,
2001

Source: youtube.com

❝

I never wanted to be a father.
I never wanted to have
children until I went to the
Ukraine on a visit for the
Elton John AIDS Foundation
with David to an orphanage.

❞

Elton John, interview with Terry Gross, 2019

Source: npr.org

Elton John and
David Furnish were
married in the UK in
2014

66

I think most heads of most
record companies are idiots
... They're only in it for
themselves. They don't care
about artists.

99

Elton John, interview with Danielle de Wolfe,
Shortlist, 2011

Source: standard.co.uk

66

I have spent most of my life fighting the AIDS pandemic, and we made great progress for two reasons: one, we've always followed the science; two, we've put our arms around everyone to make sure no one gets left behind. These same lessons apply equally to the COVID pandemic.

While most here today
have been vaccinated against
COVID, only four per cent in
Africa are. We must not leave
anyone behind.

99

Elton John, Global Citizen Live, Paris, 2021

Source: people.com

"Don't Let the Sun Go Down on Me" (1974)

♪

Originally written, with Bernie Taupin, for *Carabou*

♪

Proceeds from the 1991 single go to ten different charities

♪

George Michael and Elton first sang the song together at Live Aid in 1985

"Don't Let the Sun Go Down on Me" (1991), performed by Elton John and George Michael, was a No. 1 hit in the UK and USA.

"

Elton's often blissfully and sweetly unaware of the impact that he has with his celebrity, because he's not really a very self-centred person in that regard at all.

"

David Furnish, interview with Decca Aitkenhead, *The Guardian*, 2013

Source: theguardian.com

“

We've had the most amazing year doing stuff together, watching lots of movies, lots of television. Elton is continuing to just devour new music; he listens to everything new that comes out all the time.

”

David Furnish on the COVID-19 lockdown, interview with Richard Arnold, *Good Morning Britain*, 2021

Source: metro.co.uk

"

I used to be the shyest
person in the world and
I never, ever thought I would
become who I became.
I embraced life and seized the
adventure and began to
open up like a flower.

"

Elton John, interview with Jude Rogers, 2021

Source: theguardian.com

66

I used to be a piano player
who sang and now I'm a
singer who plays piano.

99

Elton John, 1987

Source: femalefirst.co.uk

"I Want Love" (2001)

♪

From the *Songs from the West Coast* album

♪

The video featured Robert Downey Jr in Greystone Mansion, LA

♪

The song was nominated for a Grammy in 2002

Robert Downey Jr
shot the video for
"I Want Love" in one
day (16 takes).

Source: cheatsheet.com

66

I love Australia. I love its spirit, its lack of pretence, its passion. I hope it can embrace the honesty and courage that see[k]s gay marriage as an expression not of desire but of love.

99

Elton John, 2017

Source: instagram.com

66

I wasn't a sex symbol
so I had fun with my outfits,
and I just went for it.

99

Elton John, *Carpool Karaoke*
with James Corden, 2016

Source: youtube.com

"

There's so much good music
out there. Much better than
all the pop s**t they play on
Radio 1. I never liked shows
like *The X Factor*; I'm glad
they are on the way out.

"

Elton John, interview with John Heaf,
ES Magazine, 2016

Source: standard.co.uk

146

"

My mouth tends to get me into
trouble because we live in
such a PC world.

"

Elton John, interview with Danielle de Wolfe,
Shortlist, 2011

Source: standard.co.uk

CHAPTER
FIVE

Friends

Elton is famous for his friends and feuds, as well as his razor-sharp wit. He's written, performed and recorded with many other amazing artists.

Elton John and
Eminem played
"Stan" together at the
Grammy Awards in

2001

"

And when that shit was thrown at you — about you being homophobic — I just thought, 'I'm not standing for this. It's nonsense.' I had to stand up and defend you.

"

Elton John to Eminem, 2017

Source: interviewmagazine.com

66

He's an amazing guy ...
I adore him.

99

Elton John on Eminem,
The Graham Norton Show, 2017

Source: youtube.com

66

Eminem bought me and David
matching c**k rings when we
got married.

99

Elton John, interview with Alexis Petridis, 2019

Source: theguardian.com

66

From the past, I would love to have been Elizabeth Taylor, because (a) she was f**king talented and brilliant, (b) she was beautiful, (c) she had a lot of sex, and (d) she had the most fantastic jewellery.

99

Elton John to Cara Delevingne, interview with Alexis Petridis, 2019

Source: theguardian.com

66

We're both very much
individuals; we have different
ideology. But it's that old
thread of music, man. That's
what ties us together and
always has.

99

Bernie Taupin, interview with Chris Willman, 2020

Source: variety.com

"

He once called me
'rock 'n' roll's token queen'
in an interview with *Rolling
Stone*, which I thought
was a bit snooty. He wasn't
my cup of tea. No; I wasn't his
cup of tea.

"

Elton John on David Bowie, interview with
Jonathan Heaf, *ES Magazine*, 2016

Source: standard.co.uk

"

We've always been fierce enemies ... through the years, but it's always been at a playful level. But we had the worst row, like a married couple. It went on forever.

"

Rod Stewart on Elton John, *The Harry Redknapp Show*, 2021

Source: dailymail.co.uk

Elton John and
RuPaul recorded
"Don't Go Breaking
My Heart" in
1994

>

... I got a call from Randy. He said: 'Elton John wants to do a duet with you.' I told him to hold on a minute. I ran up and down the room screaming.

"

RuPaul, interview with Laurence Watts
in *Pink News*, 2011

Source: pinknews.co.uk

66

There was always something
to take away from Joe's lyrics.
He was always trying to raise
awareness of what was going
on in the world, both socially
and politically.

99

Elton John on Joe Strummer, The Music Interview,
142 Revolution Rock, 2003

Source: epitaph.com

160

"

[Bono] was talking a lot about his early days ... Hearing about those early days in Dublin was great, as you don't often hear Bono talking about that and it made me even more fond of him.

"

Elton John on Bono, *GQ*, 2019

Source: independent.ie

66

There has never been a cool keyboard player, apart from Elton John.

99

Noel Gallagher

Source: brainyquote.com

"

George [Michael] was a late
arrival at school and he was
sort of put in my charge,
and one of the immediate
similarities was that we both
enjoyed music — specifically
Elton John.

"

Andrew Ridgeley

Source: brainyquote.com

"

[Elton John is]
a melodic genius.

"

French President Emmanuel Macron, 2019

Source: nme.com

> I've never been very interested in looking back at my career. It happened, I'm incredibly grateful, but I'm more interested in what I'm doing next rather than what I did 40 years ago.

Elton John, *The Observer*, 2019

Source: theguardian.com

Elton John Top Ten YouTube

10. "Your Song " (43m)

9. "I Guess That's Why They Call It the Blues " (58m)

8. "Don't Go Breaking My Heart (with Kiki Dee) (62m)

7. "Tiny Dancer" (84m)

6. "Nikita" (95m)

5. "Rocket Man" (101m)

4. "Sorry Seems to Be the Hardest Word " (Blue feat. Elton John) (107m)

3. "Don't Let the Sun Go Down on Me" (with George Michael) (119m)

2. "I'm Still Standing " (124m)

1. "Sacrifice " (395m)

Source: kworb.net

"

He's taken us under his wing a little bit...

"

Brandon Flowers of The Killers on Elton John, 2008

Source: KROQ-FM radio station

66

He's been my mentor
for a long time.

99

Lady Gaga on Elton John, to Zane Lowe, 2020

Source: applemusic.com

Elton wrote "I Don't Feel Like Dancin'" with the Scissor Sisters in

2006

66

He's like your
favorite grandma.

99

Jake Shears on Elton John,
interview with Seth Gorman, 2011

Source: newyorker.com

"Cold Heart (Pnau Remix)" (2021)

♪

Written by Elton John and Dua Lipa, remixed by Pnau

♪

Released on Elton's album *The Lockdown Sessions*

♪

Samples "Sacrifice", "Rocket Man", Kiss the Bride" and "Where's the Shoorah?"

> ## Ever since we first 'met' online, we totally clicked.

Dua Lipa, 2021

Source: eltonjohn.com

Collaborators/contributors on *The Lockdown Sessions*

6lack
Jimmie Allen
Glen Campbell
Brandi Carlile
Miley Cyrus
Gorillaz
SG Lewis
Lil Nas X
Dua Lipa
Yo-Yo Ma

Nicki Minaj
Stevie Nicks
Charlie Puth
Rina Sawayama
Chad Smith
Surfaces
Robert Trujillo
Years & Years
Young Thug
Eddi Vedder
Watt
Stevie Wonder

Source: wikipedia.org

"

I won't be kicking Nicki Minaj off the charts.

"

Elton John, Q&A with Bob Santelli
for *Diving Board*, 2013

Source: hollywoodreporter.com

66

I love that record!
I actually asked [Universal
Music CEO] David Joseph
about it. I heard a track
on Beats 1 and I loved it
so much.

99

Elton John on Young Thug, interview with
Sam Wolfson, *Vice*, 2016

Source: vice.com

"

... Billie Eilish, she is one
for the most talented young
ladies I've ever heard.
Her album was amazing.

"

Elton John, interview with Jacob Moore, 2019

Source: complex.com

> He was like, 'Darling, it's Elton.' I'm like, 'Elton John?' and he was like, 'You bet! Are you ready to do this interview?' and I'm like, 'Oh my gosh, I have an interview with Elton John right now.'

Charlie Puth, 2020

Source: smoothradio.com

66

I've always wanted to smash
a guitar over someone's head.
You just can't do that
with a piano.

99

Elton John, 2000

Source: brainyquote.com

"

I want to bring my songs and melodies to hip-hop beats. It may be a disaster, it could be fantastic, but you don't know until you try.

"

Elton John

Source: imdb.com

"

[Elton] has pretty much given me [normal advice] like 'keep doing you', 'be yourself' and whatnot, and he probably told me other things that I can't remember.

"

Lil Nas X, interview on 105.1 FM, 2021

Source: independent.co.uk

> **"**
>
> # A dream come true, one of the top three things I've ever done! Thank you Elton!
>
> **"**

Stevie Nicks on her duet "Stolen Cars"
with Elton John, 2021

Source: stevienicks.info

CHAPTER
SIX

Your Song

A non-exhaustive list of
Elton's main album releases.

Albums

Date indicates year of first release

Empty Sky (1969)
Elton John (1970)
Tumbleweed Connection (1970)
Madman Across the Water (1971)
Honky Château (1972)
*Don't Shoot Me I'm Only the
Piano Player* (1973)
Goodbye Yellow Brick Road (1973)
Caribou (1974)

Captain Fantastic and the
Brown Dirt Cowboy (1975)
Rock of the Westies (1975)
Blue Moves (1976)
A Single Man (1978)
Victim of Love (1979)
21 at 33 (1980)
The Fox (1981)
Jump Up! (1982)
Too Low for Zero (1983)
Breaking Hearts (1984)

Ice on Fire (1985)
Leather Jackets (1986)
Reg Strikes Back (1988)
Sleeping with the Past (1989)
The One (1992)
Made in England (1995)
The Big Picture (1997)
Songs from the West Coast (2001)
Peachtree Road (2004)
The Captain & the Kid (2006)
The Diving Board (2013)
Wonderful Crazy Night (2016)
Regimental Sgt. Zippo (2021)

Collaboration Albums

Duets (1993)

The Union (with Leon Russell) (2010)

Good Morning to the Night (with Pnau) (2012)

The Lockdown Sessions (2021)

Soundtrack Albums

Friends (1971)

The Lion King (1994)

Elton John and Tim Rice's Aida (1999)

The Muse (1999)

The Road to El Dorado (2000)

Billy Elliot the Musical (2005)

Gnomeo & Juliet (2011)

Live Albums

17-11-70 (1971)

Here and There (1976)

Live in Australia (1987)

One Night Only — The Greatest
Hits (2000)

Live from Moscow 1979 (2020)

66

I want to finish it in the right way ... I've been doing this since I was 17 – I've had enough applause. I'll be 76 when the tour finishes – who knows how much [time] I've got left? It will be spent with the kids, and with David, smelling the roses.

99

Elton John,
in an interview with Ben Beaumont-Thomas, 2021

Source: theguardian.com